INTERVENTION

Decodable Multi-syllable Phonics Unit

Compound Words with VCe

The Science of Reading for Older Students

Phonics Workbook for Older Students Multi-Syllable Word Unit V/CV. December 2022

ISBN: 9798367292787

Decodable Multisyllable Words Set 3

Research Based

Why Fluency?

To be considered "on level" in reading fluency, students should be able to read aloud an unrehearsed passage, (i.e., either narrative or expository, fiction or non-fiction that is 200 to 300 words in length) from a grade-level text, with at least 95% accuracy in word reading. As students read aloud, their reading should sound as effortless as if they were speaking (Hasbrouck & Glaser, 2012.) This does not come easily for some students, which is why fluency practice is so essential.

In order to be considered fluent readers, students in grades 9 through 12 should be able to correctly read 150 words per minute (Hasbrouck & Tindal, 2006). In 2006 and again in 2010, Hasbrouck and Hasbrouck & Tindal (respectively) put forth that "[i]t is sufficient for students to read unpracticed, grade-level text at the 50th percentile of oral reading fluency norms" and that "…teachers do not need to have students read faster because there is no evidence that reading faster than the 50th percentile increases comprehension." See chart below.

The best strategy for developing and improving reading fluency is to provide students with many opportunities to read the same passages orally several times. These exercises provide such opportunities. On each passage, there is space for reading fluency calculations. The best part is that the passages are quick and make it easy for students to read aloud repeatedly – and often – without taking up a lot of valuable classroom time. The activities can also be spread over several days.

Grade	Percentile	Fall WPM	Winter WPM	Spring WPM		Grade	Percentile	Fall WPM	Winter WPM	Spring WPM
1	90		81	111		5	90	166	182	194
	75		47	82			75	139	156	168
	50		23	53			50	110	127	139
	25		12	28			25	85	99	109
	10		6	15			10	61	74	83
2	90	106	125	142		6	90	177	195	204
	75	79	100	117			75	153	167	177
	50	51	72	89			50	127	140	150
	25	25	42	61			25	98	111	122
	10	11	18	31			10	68	82	93
3	90	128	146	162		7	90	180	192	202
	75	99	120	137			75	156	165	177
	50	71	92	107			50	128	136	150
	25	44	62	78			25	102	109	123
	10	21	36	48			10	79	88	98
4	90	145	166	180		8	90	185	199	199
	75	119	139	152			75	161	173	177
	50	94	112	123			50	133	146	151
	25	68	87	98			25	106	115	125
	10	45	61	72			10	77	84	97

These passages are designed for older students who are very low readers.

This programs works for resource, whole class, RTI, and summer school. If you are using this program with more than one student – partner up. Partnering students is engaging and lets everyone participate. I find that students helping students builds confidence and reinforces learning; additionally, by reading, tracking and reading again, student exposure to each passage is maximized. Research suggests that pairing readings with like-level reading partners is motivating and increases reading success.

Instruction for Group, Whole Class, or Zoom Fluency Practice

Before you begin, have a copy of one passage for each student. The PDF can be displayed before the whole class on a Smartboard or printed and projected on a document camera. As you explain the lessons, demonstrate what students will be doing.

Explain what fluency is - the rate and ease at which we read along with the flow of reading.

Break students into pairs and hand out one copy per student. If you are working with a group of students with varying abilities - pair like-leveled students together.

Explain the entire activity, as well as how to calculate combined words per minute, or CWPM. Then read the passage aloud. Have students track on their sheets as you read aloud. It is extremely beneficial for struggling students to hear the passage before they read it aloud. The goal isn't to have students stumble, but to optimize opportunities for ultimate success.

The first few times you do fluency as a class – the script below may be helpful:

1. **Check to make sure each person is in the right spot and then read the passage.**
2. **After you read the selected passage aloud, partner students and say something like:** *Put your name on your paper. Since you need to be marking your partner's paper, switch papers now. Raise your hand if you are Partner 1.*
3. **Pause until one student from each pair has their hand raised – acknowledge students when one person of each pair has their hand raised.**
4. **Raise your hand if you are Partner 2.** Pause until the other student from each pair has their hand raised – acknowledge students when the other partner has their hand raised.

   Excellent. When I say "Begin", all Partner 1s should quietly begin to read to their partners.

   All Partner 2s will use their pencils to keep track of their partner's errors. Partner 2s will put a line over each word pronounced incorrectly.

   When the timer goes off, all Partner 2s will circle the last word read, but Partner 1s will keep reading until the passage is complete. Does anyone have any questions?

5. **Set the timer for two minutes. If there are no questions -** *Begin.*
6. **When the timer goes off:** *Partner 2s, please mark your partner's score and give feedback to Partner 1s.*
7. **Walk around the room to make sure scores are being marked correctly.**
8. **Make sure students are ready and then switch for Partner 2s to read.**

   Ready? Begin.

Multisyllabic Word Reading Research

To progress in reading, students must have strategies for decoding big words. From fifth grade on, the average student encounters about 10,000 new words each year. Most of these words are multisyllabic. (Nagy and Anderson 1984).

It is helpful for students to be familiar with the common rules for syllable division. Knowing these rules and being able to apply them flexibly will help students decode longer multisyllabic words. (Carreker 2005; Henry 2010b)

According to Shefelbine and Calhoun 1991, "Low decoders, correctly pronounced fewer affixes and vowel sounds, disregarded large portions of letter information and were two to four times more likely to omit syllables."

Several studies have shown that teaching students strategies for decoding longer words improves their decoding ability. (Archer et al. 2006; Archer 2018.)

To Recognize a Decoding Problem – Look for these Symptoms:
- Guessing at words from context
- Avoiding sounding out new words
- Confusing similar sounds, symbols, and/or words
- Inaccurate reading of nonsense words or words out of context
- Inadequate sight word vocabulary
- Tires easily, looks away, is easily frustrated, hates to read

These strategies build word recognition and build strong readers:
- Phonemic Awareness
- Vocabulary/Morphology
- Fluency

Teaching Syllabication
- Syllabication instruction teaches a struggling reader strategies to decode multisyllable words quickly.

- Students learn to systematically break a multisyllable word into small manageable syllables, identify the vowel sounds within each syllable and "sound out" the word syllable by syllable.

- As students progress through the lessons, they will internalize the process and apply it easily and effortlessly.

- Students will become faster, more efficient, and fluent readers who comprehend at a higher level.

Teacher Page

Multisyllable Words Rule 4: Compound VCe

V stands for vowel, C stands for consonant, and e is the silent e at the end of a syllable or word. The VCe syllable pattern works just like the silent e rule. **A VCe syllable pattern ends in silent e, which makes the vowel before it a long sound** (it says its name). Examples include stripe, shine, bake.

Word	Correct	Word	Correct
backfire		hillside	
backslide		inside	
bedtime		lifelong	
campfire		lifetime	
campsite		notepad	
cupcake		pancake	
fireman		pipeline	
fireside		pothole	
flagpole		shipmate	
frostbite		spaceship	
grapevine		springtime	
homemade		stovepipe	
homesick		sunrise	

Student Page

Multisyllable Words Rule 4: Compound VCe

V stands for vowel, C stands for consonant, and e is the silent e at the end of a syllable or word. The VCe syllable pattern works just like the silent e rule. **A VCe syllable pattern ends in silent e, which makes the vowel before it a long sound** (it says its name). Examples include stripe, shine, bake.

Word	Word
backfire	hillside
backslide	inside
bedtime	lifelong
campfire	lifetime
campsite	notepad
cupcake	pancake
fireman	pipeline
fireside	pothole
flagpole	shipmate
frostbite	spaceship
grapevine	springtime
homemade	stovepipe
homesick	sunrise

VCe Compound Words

Multisyllable Words Rule: Compound VCe

V stands for vowel

C stands for consonant

e is the silent e at the end of a syllable or word.

The VCe syllable pattern works just like the silent e rule.

A VCe syllable pattern ends in silent e. This makes the vowel before it a long sound

The vowel says its name.
Examples include stripe, shine, bake.

back/fire

fire/man

life/long

space/ship

backfire

fireman

lifelong

spaceship

backfire

fireman

lifelong

spaceship

backfire

fireman

lifelong

spaceship

backfire

fireman

lifelong

spaceship

VCe Compound Words

Find each word twice.

Word Search

```
U L T C U C W J T U A W E T S
L I H Y L I B A C K F I R E U
I F R H J X P I J L H H X W N     Word Bank:
F E L I A W D S U N R I S E R
E L K F D A Y L L D P M B W I     backfire
L O F L A G P O L E Y B W F S     fireman
O N X G S P A C E S H I P I E     lifelong
N G S P A C E S H I P X G R H     spaceship
G P T V P O T H O L E O P E I     hillside
B A C K F I R E V R B N O M L     sunrise
F I R E M A N U W D V I T A L     flagpole
W U N W F L A G P O L E H N S     pothole
K X F O I R R Z M T O I O K I
H I L L S I D E H Q H O L N D
Y R X S G M O S I A K O E C E
```

Write two sentences using: backfire, fireman, lifelong, and spaceship.

_____

_____

_____

_____

_____

_____

_____

_____

ACROSS

2. I have known her for so long. We are ___ friends.
4. The ___ touched down on the space station.
5. Put the flag up the ___.
7. The ___ was beautifully orange this morning.

DOWN

1. The fireman set a ___ to try to save the forest.
3. The flowers were growing up the ___
5. The ___ saved the people from the burning building.
6. The jeep bumped into the ___.

Sentence Fluency: VCe Compound Words

The fireman saved the forest.	06
The fireman started a backfire.	11
The fireman saved the forest by starting a backfire.	18
Saving the forest with a backfire was the fireman's idea.	29
He was a lifelong fireman.	34
He was a lifelong lover of the forest.	43
The fireman did not start the fire.	54
A spaceship started the fire.	59
A spaceship landed in the forest.	65
The spaceship exploded.	73
The fireman saw the spaceship explode.	78
The other firemen saw the spaceship explode.	86
The backfire helped the firemen put out the fire.	93
I am a lifelong believer of backfires.	99
A backfire is a tool used by firemen.	112
They light a backfire to burn towards the fire.	124
The backfire helps firemen save forests.	130
The spaceship carried the fireman.	141
It was his lifelong dream to fly in a spaceship.	149
His lifelong dream caused a fire.	155
Luckily, he was a fireman.	164
Luckily, he was a fireman who could set a backfire.	170

Words Read: _____ minus mistakes: _____ equals wpms: _____	Words Read: _____ minus mistakes: _____ equals wpms: _____	Words Read: _____ minus mistakes: _____ equals wpms: _____
Words Read: _____ minus mistakes: _____ equals wpms: _____	Words Read: _____ minus mistakes: _____ equals wpms: _____	Words Read: _____ minus mistakes: _____ equals wpms: _____

Fluency: VCe Compound Words

"It is my lifelong dream to be a fireman," Tim said. "It is my lifelong dream to	17
save forests."	19
"You want to be a forest fireman?" Dad asked.	28
"Yes, I do want to be a forest fireman. I also want to be a spaceship	44
fireman."	45
Dad laughed. "What is a spaceship fireman? That sounds like something you	57
made up."	59
Tim laughed too. "No, I saw it on YouTube. It's real. Spaceship firemen are	73
real."	74
"I know I will regret asking. What does a spaceship fireman do?"	86
"A spaceship fireman puts out fires in space. Duh!" Tim said.	97
"How? With what?" Dad asked. "And where? Where in space do these	109
spaceship firemen work?"	112
"Well, fires can't start in space. They do start on spaceships. There was this	126
spaceship fireman. He tried to set a backfire on the spaceship. The whole thing	140
blew up."	142
"That's insane," Dad said. "Doesn't seem like there would be much need.	154
How many spaceships are going to need firemen?"	162
"Not a lot," Tim said. "I guess I should stick to setting backfires in the forest."	178
"Well, no setting backfires in the forest until you are a fireman."	190
"That would be a given," Tim said as he walked out the door.	203
"Where are you going?" Dad asked.	209
"To practice setting fires in the firepit."	216
"Please, no backfires," Dad said. "Please, please no backfires."	225

Words Read: _____ minus mistakes: _____ equals wpms: _____	Words Read: _____ minus mistakes: _____ equals wpms: _____	Words Read: _____ minus mistakes: _____ equals wpms: _____
Words Read: _____ minus mistakes: _____ equals wpms: _____	Words Read: _____ minus mistakes: _____ equals wpms: _____	Words Read: _____ minus mistakes: _____ equals wpms: _____

Cloze Read: VCe Compound Words

Directions: Chose the correct compound CVe words to fill in the blanks.

"It is my lifelong dream to be a fireman," Tim said. "It is my _____ dream to save forests."

"You want to be a forest _____ ?" Dad asked.

"Yes, I do want to be a forest fireman. I also want to be a spaceship fireman."

Dad laughed. "What is a _____ fireman? That sounds like something you made up."

Tim laughed too. "No, I saw it on YouTube. It's real. Spaceship firemen are real."

"I know I will regret asking. What does a _____ fireman do?"

"A spaceship fireman puts out fires in space. Duh!" Tim said.

"How? With what?" Dad asked. "And where? Where in space do these spaceship firemen work?"

"Well, fires can't start in space. They do start on spaceships. There was this spaceship fireman. He tried to set a _____ on the spaceship. The whole thing blew up."

"That's insane," Dad said. "Doesn't seem like there would be much need. How many spaceships are going to need _____ ?"

"Not a lot," Tim said. "I guess I should stick to setting backfires in the forest."

"Well, no setting _____ in the forest until you are a fireman."

"That would be a given," Tim said as he walked out the door.

"Where are you going?" Dad asked.

"To practice setting fires in the _____ ."

"Please, no backfires," Dad said. "Please, please no backfires."

VCe fireman, backfire, spaceship, lifelong

Directions: Please select the best response.

1. Tim wants to
   a. be a spaceman.
   b. be a fireman.
   c. be a dad.
   d. fly to space.

2. Who asks what a space fireman does?
   a. Tim
   b. Dad
   c. Mom
   d. no one

3. What happened when the spaceship fireman tried to set a backfire in space?
   a. it wouldn't start
   b. he was sent to the forest
   c. he blew up the spaceship
   d. nothing

4. Who has the lifelong dream of being a fireman?
   a. Dad
   b. Mom
   c. Tom
   d. Tim

5. What does dad think is insane?
   a. blowing up a spaceship with a backfire
   b. setting backfires
   c. flying to space
   d. watching YouTube

6. It is Tim's lifelong dream to
   a. save space
   b. fly in spaceships
   c. save forests
   d. set backfires

7. Put a line through the syllable break.

Example: back/fire

b a c k f i r e

f i r e m a n

l i f e l o n g

s p a c e s h i p

f i r e m e n

8. VCe – Rewrite the rule in your own words:

Multisyllable Words Rule 4: Compound VCe

V stands for vowel, C stands for consonant, and e is the silent e at the end of a syllable or word. The VCe syllable pattern works just like the silent e rule. **A VCe syllable pattern ends in silent e, which makes the vowel before it a long sound** (It says its name). Examples include stripe, shine, bake.

_____

_____

_____

_____

_____

_____

_____

_____

_____

_____

1

Instructions: Cut along the solid lines. Fold along the dotted lines. Write the words showing the syllable break. Color and decorate.

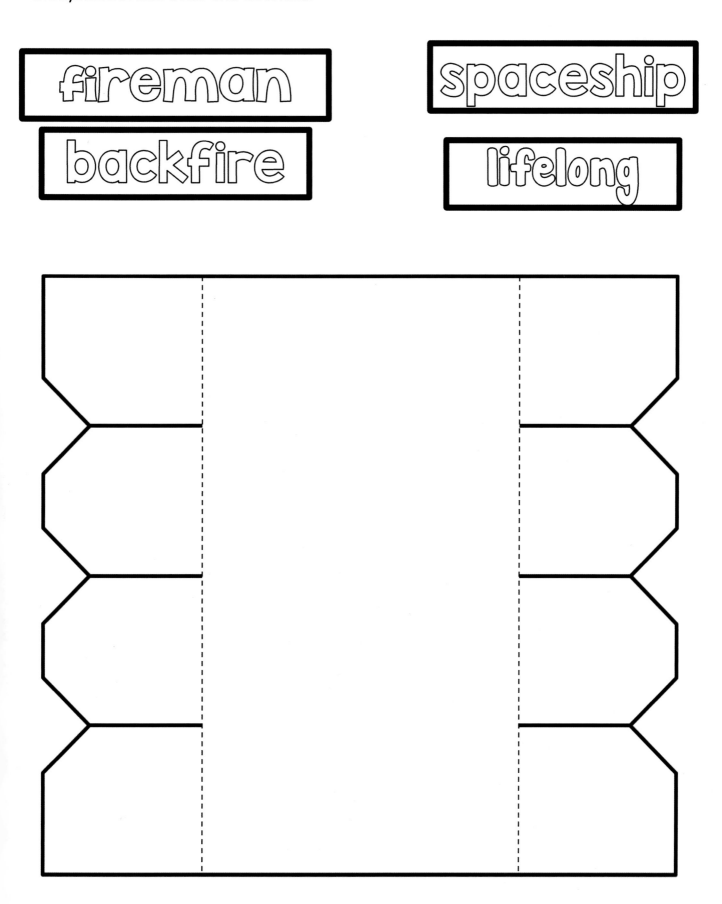

VCe Compound Words

hill/side

sun/rise

flag/pole

pot/hole

hillside

pothole

sunrise

flagpole

flagpole

hillside

pothole

sunrise

hillside

Word Search

```
D S T J F R O S T B I T E B Q
H I L L S I D E S U N R I S E
H I U F U Y S P A C E S H I P
S P A C E S H I P X H Q U B A
V Y O Q P F D B A C K F I R E
I L T I E I R F D Q T U N U B
I A H M I B P O L E C A U P A
H I L L S I D E S A G B T O C
P I P E L I N E L T G U D T K
G R A P E V I N E I B P W H F
N O T E P A D G B W N I O O I
T E T P S U N R I S E E T L R
H N N E M G R A P E V I N E E
H S X N K L I F E L O N G N A
B W C L S C L I F E L O N G S
```

Word Bank:

hillside
sunrise
flagpole
pothole
backfire
lifelong
spaceship
frostbite
grapevine
pipeline
notepad

DOWN

1. The car hit the ____ on the road.
3. The gas ____ runs from Alaska to Oregon.
4. The fireman set a ____ to stop the forest fire.
6. She is my ____ friend.
7. They rode in the ____ to Mars.
8. The flowers grew all along the ____.

ACROSS

2. Take notes on the ____.
5. The ____ was golden and beautiful this morning.
9. I heard it through the ____. It is also a fruit plant.
10. Take the flag off of the ____ at dusk.
11. The hiker got ____ when he walked in the snow without shoes.

Sentence Fluency: hillside, sunrise, flagpole, and pothole

The flowers were on the hillside.	06
We sat on the hillside to watch the sunrise.	15
We sat on the hillside and put the flag up the flagpole.	27
At sunrise we raised the flag up the flagpole.	36
The road we took to the flagpole had potholes.	45
We drove our car through the potholes.	52
We watched the sunrise on the hillside.	59
After we hit the pothole, we stopped.	66
After we hit the pothole, we stopped and watched the sunrise.	77
After we hit the pothole, we stopped and watched the sunrise from the hillside.	91
We watched the sunrise from the hillside.	98
We watched the sunrise from the hillside while sitting under the flagpole.	110
After sunrise, we left the hillside.	116
After sunrise, we left the flagpole.	122
The house was on the hillside.	128
The road to the house has a large pothole.	137
A flagpole caused the pothole.	142
The flagpole fell.	150
Just before sunrise, we heard a loud boom.	158
It was the flagpole falling.	163
We had to get a truck to move the flagpole.	173
And there it was – a pothole in the street.	182

Words Read: _____ minus mistakes: _____ equals wpms: _____	Words Read: _____ minus mistakes: _____ equals wpms: _____	Words Read: _____ minus mistakes: _____ equals wpms: _____
Words Read: _____ minus mistakes: _____ equals wpms: _____	Words Read: _____ minus mistakes: _____ equals wpms: _____	Words Read: _____ minus mistakes: _____ equals wpms: _____

Fluency: hillside, sunrise, flagpole, and pothole

"We're putting up the flagpole today," John said.	08
"Then you'll be an eagle," Ash said. Ash was John's best friend. She'd	21
helped him raise the money for the flagpole. "It's a cool project. Who knew	35
flagpoles were so expensive?"	39
"Six grand – just for the pole. But now the park has a flagpole," John said.	54
"And a bench and pretty flowers all around it," Ash said.	65
"Don't forget the solar light that comes on at sunset," John said.	77
"Does it go off at sunrise? Does the power last that long?"	89
"It is supposed to. We'll see."	95
"The best thing is you fixed the potholes as well."	105
"That's how the whole thing started," John said. "I remember being at that	118
park from sunrise to sunset on Saturday. Those potholes caused many sprained	130
ankles."	131
John and Ash left for the park at sunrise. They waked over the hillside. The	146
truck with the lift was already there.	153
"Thanks for coming guys," John shook their hands. "I appreciate your help."	165
"This is a great thing for the town. I was a Scout. Glad to do it," Mr. Denny	183
said. He got on the truck while his son guided the placement of the flagpole.	198
Ash put on her gloves. She started planting flowers.	207
By noon, the flagpole was up. The flowers were planted. The flag raised.	220
"I thought you were waiting for the ceremony to raise the first flag?"	233
"Nah, that isn't until sunrise tomorrow. Looks good huh?"	242
"Looks great. Nice work buddy."	247

Words Read: _____ minus mistakes: _____ equals wpms: _____	Words Read: _____ minus mistakes: _____ equals wpms: _____	Words Read: _____ minus mistakes: _____ equals wpms: _____
Words Read: _____ minus mistakes: _____ equals wpms: _____	Words Read: _____ minus mistakes: _____ equals wpms: _____	Words Read: _____ minus mistakes: _____ equals wpms: _____

Cloze Read: VCe Compound Words

Directions: Chose the correct compound CVe words to fill in the blanks.

"We're putting up the _____ today," John said.

"Then you'll be an eagle," Ash said. Ash was John's best friend. She'd helped him raise the money for the flagpole. "It's a cool project. Who knew _____ were so expensive?"

"Six grand – just for the pole. But now the park has a flagpole," John said.

"And a bench and pretty flowers all around it," Ash said.

"Don't forget the solar light that comes on at _____ ," John said.

"Does it go off at sunrise? Does the power last that long?"

"It is supposed to. We'll see."

"The best thing is you fixed the _____ as well."

"That's how the whole thing started," John said. "I remember being at that park from _____ to sunset on Saturday. Those potholes caused many sprained ankles."

John and Ash left for the park at sunrise. They waked over the _____ . The truck with the lift was already there.

"Thanks for coming guys," John shook their hands. "I appreciate your help."

"This is a great thing for the town. I was a Scout. Glad to do it," Mr. Denny said. He got on the truck while his son guided the placement of the _____ .

Ash put on her gloves. She started planting flowers.

By noon, the _____ was up. The flowers were planted. The flag raised.

"I thought you were waiting for the ceremony to raise the first flag?"

"Nah, that isn't until _____ tomorrow. Looks good huh?"

"Looks great. Nice work buddy."

VCe fireman, backfire, spaceship, lifelong

Directions: Please select the best response.

1. What is at the bottom of the flagpole?
   a.   flowers and a bench
   b.   cement
   c.   bricks
   d.   bushes and flowers

2. Who helped John raise money?
   a.   Mr. Denny
   b.   Mr. Denny's son
   c.   John's troop
   d.   Ash

3. What did John fix at the park?
   a.   a broken ankle
   b.   a broken flagpole
   c.   potholes
   d.   sandboxes

4. What do Ash and John talk about being expensive?
   a.   flags
   b.   rocks
   c.   sandboxes
   d.   flagpoles

5. "By ____ the flagpole was up."
   a.   noon
   b.   sunrise
   c.   sunset
   d.   nightfall

6. Put the statements in the order in which they occur in the reading.
   a.   John shook Mr. Denny's hand
   b.   Ash put on her gloves
   c.   John and Ash walked to the park
   d.   John tells Ash the flagpole if going up

7. Put a line through the syllable break.

Example: back/fire

b a c k f i r e

f i r e m a n

l i f e l o n g

s p a c e s h i p

f i r e m e n

h i l l s i d e

s u n r i s e

f l a g p o l e

p o t h o l e

_____ _____ _____ _____

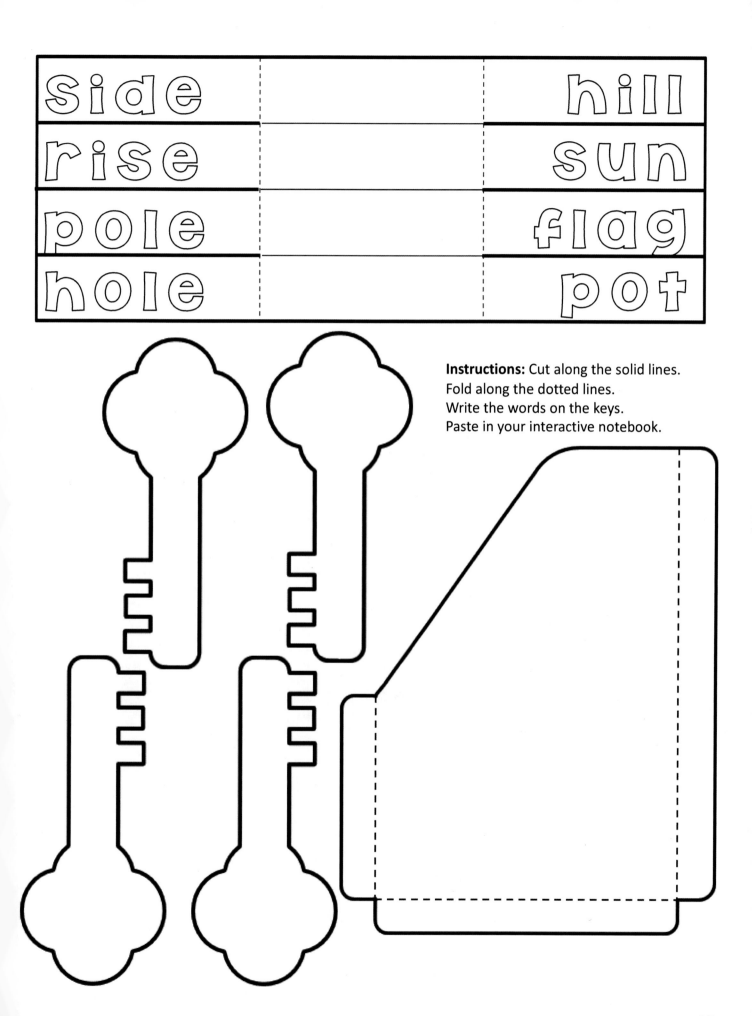

side		hill
rise		sun
pole		flag
hole		pot

Instructions: Cut along the solid lines.
Fold along the dotted lines.
Write the words on the keys.
Paste in your interactive notebook.

Kingda Ka

The fastest roller coaster in the United States is Kingda Ka. Kingda Ka is at Six Flags Great Adventures. Six Flags Great Adventures is in Jackson, New Jersey. It is the second ever strata coaster.

A strata coaster is a type of roller coaster with a height or drop of at least 400 feet. The coaster goes 128 mph. It goes from 0 to 128 in 3.5 seconds. Riders climb to 456 feet. They drop 418 feet. Sounds a bit frightening.

Manufacturer: Intamin
Product: Accelerator Coaster
Type: Steel-Launched-Strata
Riders per train: 20
Hourly capacity: 1400
Height: 456 feet
Drop: 418 feet
Speed: 128 mph
Length: 3118 feet
Drop angle: 90 degrees
Time to ride: 0:28'
G-Force: 5 g

Other Roller Coaster Facts

- The fastest coaster in the world goes 149.1 mph. It is called **Formula Rossa**. It is in the United Arab Emirates.
- **Top Thrill Dragster** is at Cedar Point in Ohio. It is a theme coaster. It goes 120 mph.
- **Superman: Escape from Krypton** has an incredible 415-foot-tall tower. It goes 100 mph. It is at Six Flags Magic Mountain in California.
- The fastest (and tallest) coaster in Canada is **Leviathan**. It is near Toronto.
- The Intimidator at **King's Dominion** reaches 90-miles-per-hour. It has a 300-foot drop at an 85-degree angle.

Roller Coaster Posts

Use the information from the reading and the VCe words to create two Instagram posts below the photos.

♡ ◯ ▽   🔖

comment

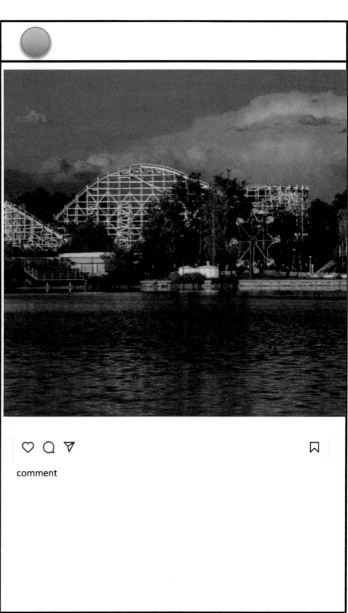

♡ ◯ ▽   🔖

comment

VCe Compound Words

camp/site

bed/time

fire/side

camp/fire

campsite

bedtime

fireside

campfire

bedtime

campsite

campfire

fireside

campsite

bedtime

fireside

campfire

bedtime

campsite

campfire

fireside

Word Search

```
T T H X M D V L R C A J B U K
Z P W F E J S F Q A Q A L A A
O H F I K H Q L Z M A C I Q L
T C X R F C S A J P K A F X Q
S A C E I M B G H F V P E N B
J M F M R Q E P I I I O L G B
I P I A E T D O L R I T O V E
A S R N S X T L L E I H N F M
A I E Q I C I E S H I O G W R
R T M Q D U M Q I U D L M W A
F E E L E Q E E D D M E G Q K
T V N B I S K S E A O T U M V
C L L S P A C E S H I P Y Q H
A S U N R I S E Q S S A S Q B
D B A C K F I R E R A X D O E
```

Word Bank:
backfire
fireman
lifelong
spaceship
firemen
hillside
sunrise
flagpole
pothole
campsite
bedtime
fireside
campfire

Write two sentences using: bedtime, campfire, campsite, fireside.

_____

_____

_____

_____

_____

_____

_____

_____

ACROSS

4. Jay wants to fly in a ____ to Mars
5. The flowers were growing up the ____.
6. The road crew fixed the ____.
7. Put the flag up the ____.
9. ____ this morning is at 5:30 a.m.
10. The ____ saved the cat from the tree.
11. Light the c__ and we will tell ghost stories.

DOWN

1. We chose a ____ by the water.
2. The firemen set a ____ to push back the blaze.
3. We will be ____ friends.
7. We sat by the ____ and made s'mores.
8. My ____ is at ten p.m.

Sentence Fluency: VCe Compound Words – campsite, bedtime, fireside, campsite

Juan and Marco found a campsite.	06
They found a campsite and built a campfire.	14
They made s'mores by the campfire.	20
They loved their campsite.	24
Bedtime came fast.	27
Bedtime under the stars came fast.	33
Bedtime at the campsite came fast.	38
Suri and Charlotte sat fireside.	43
They sat fireside at their campsite.	49
They fried the fish they caught on the campfire.	58
Bedtime came fast at Suri and Charlotte's campsite as well.	68
The four met by Juan and Marco's campsite.	76
They met and sat fireside.	87
The four were lifelong friends and had lots to talk about.	98
They talked by the campfire until someone else came.	106
It was a fireman.	110
He was camping too and told them he saw a spaceship.	121
He noticed their campsites and wondered if they saw it too.	132
They asked the fireman to sit by their campfire.	141
The fireman sat fireside and told them about spaceships.	150
They had fun at the campsite.	156
Bedtime came.	158
They all went to their campsites and went to bed.	168

Words Read: _____ minus mistakes: _____ equals wpms: _____	Words Read: _____ minus mistakes: _____ equals wpms: _____	Words Read: _____ minus mistakes: _____ equals wpms: _____
Words Read: _____ minus mistakes: _____ equals wpms: _____	Words Read: _____ minus mistakes: _____ equals wpms: _____	Words Read: _____ minus mistakes: _____ equals wpms: _____

VCe Compound Words – campsite, bedtime, fireside, campsite

"You choose the campground. Seth is picking the campsite," Mom said.	11
"I'm so excited. I love Yosemite!" Seth said. "I want to stay in one of those	27
tent cabins."	29
"That isn't camping. Besides, I have to choose the campground first. I may	42
not choose a campground with tent cabins." Suri said. "I choose Upper Pines.	55
We'll have to bring our own tents."	62
"Can we have a campfire at Upper Pines? I want to relax fireside. Some	76
campsites don't let you have campfires."	82
"Yes, it says campfires are allowed at any time," Suri said.	93
"Wow! That's odd for California," Dad said.	100
"Well, if you think about it," Seth said, "not many forest fires are started by	115
campfires."	116
They left for Upper Lakes the next morning. Yosemite was beautiful. They got	129
to their campsite. Dad unpacked the firewood. Mom built the campfire. Suri and	142
Seth put up the tent.	147
They ate dinner sitting fireside. They cooked veggie hotdogs over the	158
campfire.	159
Bedtime came too fast. They stomped out the campfire. They put away their	172
food. They went to bed.	177
The next day, they hiked up Nevada Falls. They took photos by half dome.	191
Suri even got fries from a snack shack.	199
They had a great vacation; Yosemite is their number one place to go.	212

Words Read: _____ minus mistakes: _____ equals wpms: _____	Words Read: _____ minus mistakes: _____ equals wpms: _____	Words Read: _____ minus mistakes: _____ equals wpms: _____
Words Read: _____ minus mistakes: _____ equals wpms: _____	Words Read: _____ minus mistakes: _____ equals wpms: _____	Words Read: _____ minus mistakes: _____ equals wpms: _____

Cloze Read: VCe Compound Words

Directions: Chose the correct compound CVe words to fill in the blanks.

"You choose the campground. Seth is picking the _____," Mom said.

"I'm so excited. I love Yosemite!" Seth said. "I want to stay in one of those tent cabins."

"That isn't camping. Besides, I have to choose the campground first. I may not choose a campground with tent cabins." Suri said. "I choose Upper Pines. We'll have to bring our own tents."

"Can we have a _____ at Upper Pines? I want to relax _____. Some campsites don't let you have campfires."

"Yes, it says _____ are allowed at any time," Suri said.

"Wow! That's odd for California," Dad said.

"Well, if you think about it," Seth said, "not many forest fires are started by _____."

They left for Upper Lakes the next morning. Yosemite was beautiful. They got to their _____. Dad unpacked the firewood. Mom built the campfire. Suri and Seth put up the tent.

They ate dinner sitting fireside. They cooked veggie hotdogs over the campfire. _____ came too fast. They stomped out the campfire. They put away their food. They went to bed.

The next day, they hiked up Nevada Falls. They took photos by half dome. Suri even got fries from a snack shack.

They had a great vacation; Yosemite is their number one place to go.

VCe - campfire, bedtime, fireside, campsite

Directions: Please select the best response.

1. Who gets to choose the campground?
   a. Seth
   b. Suri
   c. Mom
   d. Dad

2. Who unpacks the firewood?
   a. Seth
   b. Suri
   c. Mom
   d. Dad

3. What is the name of the campground?
   a. Lower Lakes
   b. Upper Lakes
   c. Lower Yosemite
   d. Upper Yosemite

4. What did they cook on the first night?
   a. hamburgers
   b. veggie burgers
   c. hotdogs
   d. veggie hotdogs

5. Where did the hike on the second day of their trip?
   a. Yosemite Falls
   b. Upper Lakes Falls
   c. Lower Lakes Falls
   d. Nevada Falls

6. Put the statements in the order they appear in the reading
   a. The family hikes to Nevada Falls
   b. They decide on a campground
   c. They eat dinner fireside
   d. Seth chooses a campsite

   _____ _____ _____ _____

7. Put a line through the syllable break.

Example: pot/hole

backfire

fireman

lifelong

spaceship

firemen

hillside

sunrise

flagpole

pothole

campfire

bedtime

fireside

campsite

VCe Compound Words

fire
time
side
site

camp
bed
fire
camp

Instructions: Cut along the solid lines. Fold along the dotted lines. Color and decorate. Paste in your interactive notebook.

VCe Compound Words

cup|cak_e_

in|sid_e_

spring|tim_e_

hom_e_|mad_e_

pan|cak_e_

cupcake homemade
pancake inside
inside homemade
cupcake SPRINGTIME
pancake homemade
SPRINGTIME inside
pancake cupcake
inside SPRINGTIME
cupcake homemade
pancake SPRINGTIME

Name: _____ Number: _____

Write two sentences using:
homesick, cupcake,
pancake, inside, springtime.

_____

_____

_____

_____

_____

_____

_____

_____

Word Search

```
C D X Y O F I R E S I D E X V
U S P A C E S H I P P I R U F
P Z L K G H I L L S I D E M E
C E L Z W D C A M P S I T E U
A P M H Z H U B E I F V Y M A
K S B Y O H A B D N I C D F E
E K P E B M B U F S R A L I F
P Q Z R D A E T Q I E M I R L
S O W B I T C S U D M P F E A
D U T I E N I K I E E F E M G
T B N H E L G M F C N I L A P
F Z W R O G F T E I K R O N O
Z N Y C I L S T I Q R E N W L
G R M Y Z S E V C M M E G T E
P A N C A K E U F M E F V T S
```

Word Bank:
backfire
fireman
lifelong
spaceship
firemen
hillside
sunrise
flagpole
pothole
campfire
bedtime
fireside
campsite
cupcake
inside
springtime
homesick
pancake

ACROSS
3. Roast the hotdogs over the ____.
6. The ____ landed on the moon.
7. The car bumped over the ____.
9. Come ____ and eat your cupcakes.
10. The fireman set a ____ to stop the flames.
12. We love sitting ____ and drinking hot chocolate
15. ____ are little cakes.
16. I love ____ and maple syrup.
17. ____ is at 6:30 a.m.

DOWN
1. The ____ was right by the lake.
2. The ____ was full of blooming flowers.
4. We will be ____ friends.
5. In the ____ flowers are in bloom.
8. Run the flag up the ____.
11. At camp, I got ____ and wanted to see my family.
12. The ____ set a backfire to stop the flames.
13. The ____ fought the fire.
14. Our ____ is 10 o'clock.

38

Sentence Fluency: VCe – cupcake, inside, springtime, homemade, pancake

The cupcakes are homemade.	04
The homemade cupcakes have cream inside of them.	12
The homemade cupcakes are springtime green.	18
The pancakes are homemade.	22
The homemade pancakes have blueberries inside.	28
It is springtime.	31
In springtime, we have a cupcake picnic.	38
In springtime, we eat pink cupcakes.	44
Cupcakes and pancakes are their favorite food.	51
They love cupcakes with cream inside.	57
They don't like pancakes with cream inside.	64
They love springtime pancake picnics.	69
They love homemade pancakes and cupcakes.	75
The cupcakes were chocolate.	79
The pancakes were not chocolate.	84
Do you get tired of reading sentences about pancakes and cupcakes?	95
Wouldn't you rather eat pancakes and cupcakes?	101
Wouldn't you rather eat pancakes and cupcakes in the springtime?	111
Do you even like pancakes?	116
Do you even like cupcakes?	121
Do you like springtime?	125
What do you like inside of your cupcakes?	133
Do you like your cupcakes to be homemade?	141
Do you like your pancakes to be homemade?	149

Words Read: _____ minus mistakes: _____ equals wpms: _____	Words Read: _____ minus mistakes: _____ equals wpms: _____	Words Read: _____ minus mistakes: _____ equals wpms: _____
Words Read: _____ minus mistakes: _____ equals wpms: _____	Words Read: _____ minus mistakes: _____ equals wpms: _____	Words Read: _____ minus mistakes: _____ equals wpms: _____

Name: _____ Number: _____

Fluency: VCe – cupcake, inside, springtime, homemade, pancake

Ella looked around the kitchen. It was the studio kitchen of *The Worst Cooks*	15
in America. Her goal was to win. Her goal was to win, but she could not cook.	32
Plus, she could not bake. And today the show was about baking.	43
Ella leaned over to Liv. She met Liv backstage in the greenroom. "Looks like	57
we're making cupcakes first." Ella pointed to the counters.	66
"Ugh! My cupcakes are always dry," Liv rolled her eyes.	76
"Just make sure you add lots of butter. Or you can add lots of oil."	91
"Well," Liv laughed, "not sure I should be taking advice from you. You're here	105
too. That means you probably can't bake either!"	113
Ella laughed. "You have a point. I am more of an out of the package	128
person. This homemade stuff is hard. But I can make pancakes."	139
"At least that is something. You can make pancake cupcakes."	149
"Great idea. I can theme them springtime. Springtime pancake cupcakes."	159
"Welcome to *The Worst Chef's in the World*," Chef Ann said. "Today, we	173
have our bakeoff. You will be making some type of cake. Cupcakes or cakes of	188
any kind."	188
Liv leaned over to Ella. "Here is your shot."	198
"Sounds like pancake cupcakes it is."	204
The girls got to baking. Liv made springtime spring cake. It was not edible.	218
Ella didn't win, but her pancake cupcakes weren't horrible. At least that is	231
something.	232

Words Read: _____ minus mistakes: _____ equals wpms: _____	Words Read: _____ minus mistakes: _____ equals wpms: _____	Words Read: _____ minus mistakes: _____ equals wpms: _____
Words Read: _____ minus mistakes: _____ equals wpms: _____	Words Read: _____ minus mistakes: _____ equals wpms: _____	Words Read: _____ minus mistakes: _____ equals wpms: _____

40

Cloze Read: VCe Compound Words

Directions: Chose the correct compound CVe words to fill in the blanks.

Ella looked around the kitchen. It was the studio kitchen of *The Worst Cooks in America*. Her goal was to win. Her goal was to win, but she could not cook. Plus, she could not bake. And today the show was about baking.

Ella leaned over to Liv. She met Liv backstage in the greenroom. "Looks like we're making <u>cupcakes</u> first." Ella pointed to the counters.

"Ugh! My cupcakes are always dry," Liv rolled her eyes.

"Just make sure you add lots of butter. Or you can add lots of oil."

"Well," Liv laughed, "not sure I should be taking advice from you. You're here too. That means you probably can't bake either!"

Ella laughed. "You have a point. I am more of an out of the package person. This <u>homemade</u> stuff is hard. But I can make <u>pancakes</u>."

"At least that is something. You can make pancake <u>cupcakes</u>."

"Great idea. I can theme them springtime. Springtime <u>pancake</u> cupcakes."

"Welcome to *The Worst Chef's in the World*," Chef Ann said. "Today, we have our bakeoff. You will be making some type of cake. Cupcakes or cakes of any kind."

Liv leaned over to Ella. "Here is your shot."

"Sounds like <u>pancake</u> cupcakes it is."

The girls got to baking. Liv made <u>springtime</u> spring cake. It was not edible. Ella didn't win, but her pancake <u>cupcakes</u> weren't horrible. At least that is something.

VCe – cupcake, inside, springtime, homemade, pancake

Directions: Please select the best response.

1. What show were Ella and Liv on?
   a.   The Best Cooks in America
   b.   The Worst Bakers in America
   c.   The Worst Cooks in America
   d.   The Worst Chefs in America

2. What does Ella say would make Liv's cupcakes moist?
   a.   water and oil
   b.   butter and water
   c.   water or milk
   d.   oil and butter

3. Who says: "Welcome to The...?"
   a.   Chef Elle
   b.   Chef Ann
   c.   Chef Liv
   d.   Chef Bobby Flay

4. What does Ella make?
   a.   cupcakes.
   b.   pancakes.
   c.   springtime cupcakes.
   d.   pancake cupcakes.

5. What wasn't horrible?
   a.   cupcakes.
   b.   pancakes.
   c.   springtime cupcakes.
   d.   cupcake pancakes.

6. Put the statements in the order in which they appear in the reading.
   a.   Liv made springtime cupcakes
   b.   Ella pointed to the counters
   c.   The host welcomed them
   d.   Liv says, "Here's your shot."

   _____   _____   _____   _____

7. Put a line through the syllable break.

Example: back/fire

b a c k f i r e

f i r e m a n

l i f e l o n g

s p a c e s h i p

f i r e m e n

h i l l s i d e

s u n r i s e

f l a g p o l e

p o t h o l e

c u p c a k e

i n s i d e

s p r i n g t i m e

h o m e m a d e

p a n c a k e

c a m p f i r e

b e d t i m e

f i r e s i d e

c a m p s i t e

VCe Compound Words

springtime

homemade

pancake

inside

cupcake

Instructions: Cut along the solid lines. Fold along the dotted lines. Color and decorate. Paste in your interactive notebook.

word pocket

43

Write a Paragraph
TOPIC: Explain VCe Compound Words

Topic Sentence:	The topic tells the reader what the paragraph is about. **SAMPLE:** For words with a vowel-consonant-vowel pattern, divide after the consonant if the first vowel is short. **HING:** For this essay, you may use the sample topic sentence.
Body:	The body of your paragraph provides support for your topic.
Closing Sentence:	The closing sentence refers back to the main idea. It also offers a final point about your topic.

_____

_____

_____

_____

_____

_____

_____

_____

_____

_____

_____

_____

_____

VCe

A compound word is when two or more words are made by combining two words into a single word. Example: campfire

cup	side	
in	made	
spring	fire	
home	side	
pot	time	
bed	pole	
camp	hole	
flag	cake	

Word Bank

cupcake
inside
springtime
homemade
pothole
campfire
bedtime
Flagpole

Directions: Fill in the blanks with words from the word bank.

1. My favorite snack is a chocolate _____.

2. Come _____ from the garden and wash your hands.

3. You like summer, but I like the flowers that bloom in _____.

4. Is that _____ bread made from scratch?

5. The firetruck bumped over the _____.

6. We'll make s'mores over the _____.

7. Can I stay up past my _____ tonight, please?

8. We ran the flag up the _____.

VCe

A compound word is when two or more words are made by combining two words into a single word. Example: campfire

back	long	
fire	fire	
life	ship	
space	side	
hill	man	
sun	site	
camp	cake	
pan	rise	

Word Bank

backfire
fireman
lifelong
spaceship
hillside
sunrise
campsite
pancake

Directions: Fill in the blanks with words from the word bank.

1. Mary loves a good _____ with maple syrup.

2. We picked a _____ by the lake.

3. We left at _____ and drove all morning.

4. The flowers grew up and down th _____.

5. The astronauts flew in the _____.

6. Be a _____ learner.

7. The _____ saved the burning house.

8. The fireman set a _____ to stop the forest fire.

V C e

VCe Compound Words

VCe Compound Words

Multisyllable Words Rule
Compound VCe

V stands for vowel

C stands for consonant

e is the silent e at the end of a syllable or word.

The VCe syllable pattern works just like the silent e rule.

A VCe syllable pattern ends in silent e.
This makes the vowel before it a long sound - the vowel says its name.
Examples include – cupcake, campsite, and sunrise

backfire

fireman

lifelong

spaceship

3

backfire

fireman

lifelong

spaceship

4

48

hillside

sunrise

flagpole

pothole

hill/side

sun/rise

flag/pole

pot/hole

campsit_e_

bedtim_e_

firesid_e_

campfir_e_

camp/sit_e_

bed/tim_e_

fire/sid_e_

camp/fir_e_

50

cupcak<u>e</u>

insid<u>e</u>

springtim<u>e</u>

hom<u>e</u>mad<u>e</u>

pancak<u>e</u>

cup/cak<u>e</u>

in/sid<u>e</u>

spring/tim<u>e</u>

hom<u>e</u>/mad<u>e</u>

pan/cak<u>e</u>

cake

made

time

Fold on dashed lines

Glue Here

pan

home

bed

Cut along solid lines

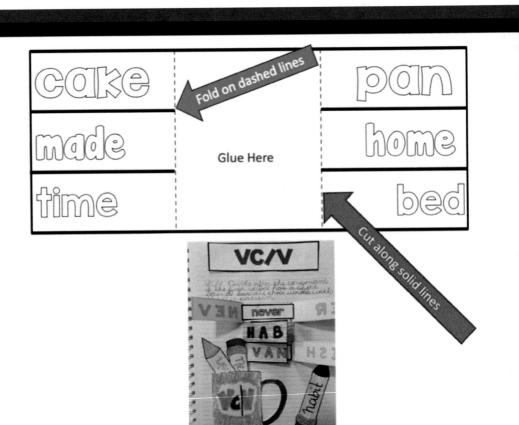

VC/V

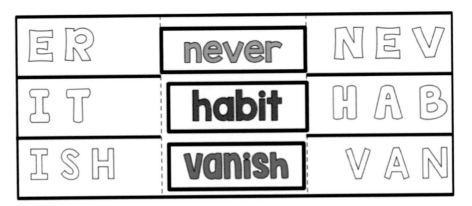

ER	never	NEV
IT	habit	HAB
ISH	vanish	VAN

Glue words in center.

5

You can decorate yours anyway you like!

Our Solar System Instagram Posts

page 12:

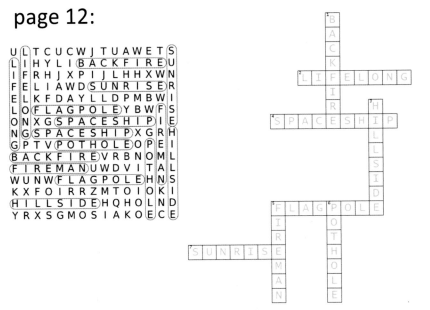

page 15:

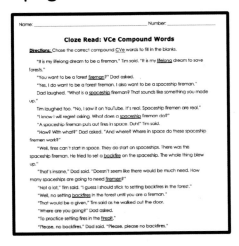

page 20:

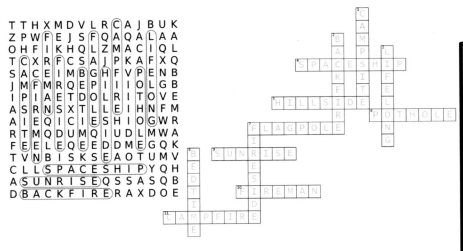

page 23:

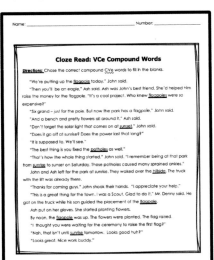

page 30:

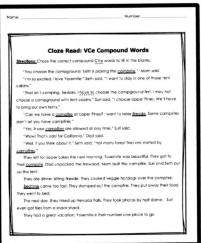

page 33:

page 38:

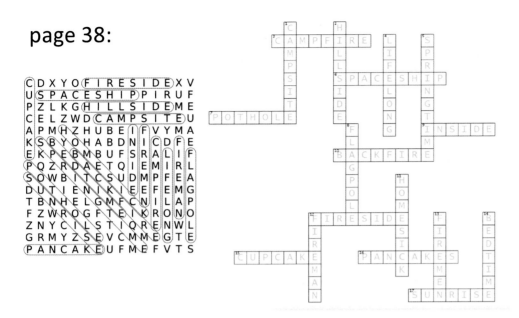

Multiple Choice Answers

page 16: 1. b; 2. b; 3. c; 4. d; 5. a; 6. c

page 24: 1. a; 2. d; 3. c; 4. d; 5. a 6. dcab

page 34: 1. b; 2. d; 3. b; 4. d; 5. d; 6. bdca

page 42: 1. c; 2. d; 3. b; 4.d 5. d 6. bcda

page 41:

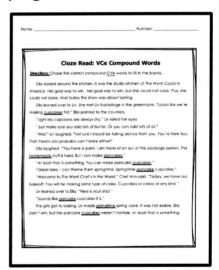

page 41:

cup	side	cupcake
in	made	inside
spring	fire	springtime
home	side	homemade
pot	time	pothole
bed	pole	bedtime
camp	hole	campfire
flag	cake	flagpole

page 42:

back	long	backfire
fire	fire	fireman
life	ship	lifelong
space	side	spaceship
hill	man	hillside
sun	site	sunrise
camp	cake	campsite
pan	rise	pancake

Credits - Clip art and fonts by:

Made in the USA
Las Vegas, NV
17 November 2024

12024642R00036